EXPLAINING AND DEFENDING AMERICAN GOVERNMENT

* * *

To a Group of Non-Americans on a Five-Hour Train Trip to Berlin

Bradley W. Rasch

iUniverse, Inc.
Bloomington

**Explaining and Defending American Government
To a Group of Non-Americans on a Five-
Hour Train Trip to Berlin**

iUniverse books may be ordered through booksellers or by contacting:

*iUniverse
1663 Liberty Drive
Bloomington, IN 47403
www.iuniverse.com
1-800-Authors (1-800-288-4677)*

*ISBN: 978-1-4759-2284-4 (sc)
ISBN: 978-1-4759-2286-8 (e)*

Library of Congress Control Number: 2012909042

Printed in the United States of America

iUniverse rev. date: 5/11/2012

THIS BOOK IS DEDICATED to all the people who love this country and seek to understand its politics and government.

Only when we must explain something near and dear to us can we fully understand it ourselves.

PREFACE

My grandfather, Albin Gustav Johnson, was born on January 4, 1885, the same day W. W. Grant of Iowa performed the first appendectomy. We were a multigenerational family; my grandfather lived with us in Hazel Crest, Illinois, from my birth in 1954 until his death.

On July 21, 1969, my grandfather was eighty-four years of age. On this day we watched Neil Armstrong take that giant leap for mankind onto the Sea of Tranquility.

To prepare me for this historic event, and to help put it into perspective for a fifteen-year-old kid, my grandfather shared with me some things about his life.

When he was a young man, he befriended an older person, a man who became a mentor of sorts to that younger version of my grandfather. This companion and mentor had been born a slave.

My grandfather recounted to me where he was on that day that will forever live in infamy, December 7, 1941. At the time he was a fifty-five-year-old worker at a steel plant in Chicago. He said he would always remember everything about that day just as clearly as he did on the day that it happened, and he said that July 21, 1969, would be the same kind of memory for me.

He spoke of the assassinations of William McKinley and JFK, his skepticism about all things Richard Nixon, and his fascination with Teddy Roosevelt (he and Teddy were young men at roughly the same time). He spoke of the Bull Moose party and LBJ's brave support of civil rights.

My grandfather certainly put things in perspective for me. He was friends with a man who had been born into slavery. My connection with that historical disgrace was living, breathing, and teaching me just before Neil Armstrong stepped onto the moon.

This is what kicked off my love of American history, politics, and government.

During the summer of 2011, I took a long train trip in Germany with a group of college professors of various nationalities. The conversation among strangers turned (as it often does when people meet Americans abroad) to American politics and government.

These fellow passengers had a great many questions about our government and how it works. My explanations to them taught me a lot about our country as well.

Sometimes you do not realize what is important, and do not fully understand it yourself, until you have to explain it to someone else.

This book is about what we discussed and their reactions to it.

INTRODUCTION

THIS BOOK IS BASED on a conversation between the author and a group of European college professors on a long train ride in Germany in 2012. Their meeting was by chance.

The conversation centered on American government and politics and the author's attempt to explain these topics while fielding questions from his fellow passengers.

Most of the topics were brought up by the European educators.

In some cases, the author researched information after the train ride so that the reader could have access to more expansive data, quotes, and other details.

Questions addressed were far ranging and were reflective of the interests of these passengers.

It is hoped that this book can serve as a primer for American students, as well as an indicator of the interests that others have in a system they want to emulate.

PRESIDENTS CAN BE (AND HAVE BEEN) ELECTED WITH FEWER POPULAR VOTES THAN THEIR OPPONENTS

✦ ✦ ✦

THERE HAVE BEEN PRESIDENTS elected with fewer popular votes than their opponents. Several presidents have been elected with less than a majority of the votes cast.

When I told my compartment companions that George Bush had received fewer popular votes than Al Gore yet won the election, they were shocked. "How did that happen?" they asked. "Are you glad that it just happened once? How could the military stand for that?"

I explained that it happened twice before Bush versus Gore. Rutherford B. Hayes and Benjamin Harrison also were elected with fewer popular votes than their main opponent.

I ordered a stiff drink before having to explain the Electoral College and why the military's feelings about the election were irrelevant.

Before I explained the Electoral College, I made them promise to explain why people in my country "run" for office and people in their countries "stand" for office. Though they promised to do so, the promise was not kept.

THE ELECTORAL COLLEGE

THE PRESIDENT AND VICE president are not elected directly by the popular vote of the people. The Electoral College elects the president and vice president. The Electoral College has no football team, no professors, no tuition, and no campus. It does not even grant degrees.

My foreign friends were shocked by this (as are some Americans). Who are these people in this Electoral College? Can they be corrupted? The answers are it depends, and it depends.

Each state has a number of electoral votes equal to its number of senators (always two from each state) plus its number of representatives in the House of Representatives, which is determined by the state's population. We have a census every ten years, which among other things determines how many representatives in the House of Representatives each state gets. There are always 435 members in the House of Representatives. How many each state gets of those 435 is determined by its population recorded during the last census.

I explained to them that my home state of Illinois has two senators (as does every state) and nineteen representatives; therefore, it has twenty-one electoral votes.

No federal regulations require an elector (what you call a member of the Electoral College) to vote for the individual that received the most votes from the people in that state. Some state laws require that they do, and other states have no such requirement. It is possible that electors could "vote their conscience" and cast their vote for someone other than the person who won the popular vote in that state.

How electors are chosen varies from state to state. Sometimes political parties choose them, and sometimes they are elected by the people.

Historically, these electors have not always voted in accordance with the popular vote of their state.

Is it possible that the electors could vote for a person who received significantly fewer votes than their opponent, therefore handing the election to someone who did not win the popular vote in any state? Possible but not likely.

The District of Columbia (Washington, DC, the nation's capital) has three electoral votes. They do not, however, have senators or representatives who can vote on the laws of the country. The people there pay taxes. So much for "No taxation without representation."

Why do we have the Electoral College? Because the founding fathers did not trust the wisdom of the masses. It was put in place as a safeguard from the whims of the people (the voters).

"Will you always have this Electoral College?" my fellow passengers asked. Yes, we probably will. You see, the Electoral College is in the Constitution, and changing the Constitution is as likely as the Chicago Cubs winning the World Series (this analogy was lost on my European friends).

To further complicate factors, the Electoral College also decides on the vice president. What if the Electoral College is gridlocked or cannot reach a decision on who should be the president and vice president? The House of Representatives decides on who the president will be, and the Senate decides the vice presidency.

The foreigners were surprised about this whole democracy thing. I was able to point out, though, that the military or the church has never intervened, and the process has always been peaceful (but not always civil).

The whole Electoral College thing came as a real surprise to these folks. "Isn't it a bit antiquated?" they asked.

"Yes," I replied, "but we hold our Constitution to be sacred."

"Are you insulted that the founding fathers did not trust you to elect a president directly?"

"No," I replied, "in my home state we elected Rod Blagojevich for governor twice, demonstrating we could not be trusted with the vote."

"Who was he?" they asked.

"You do not want to know" was my firm reply, which ended their questions on that matter. He went to prison on 3/15, becoming inmate 40892-424, at Federal Correctional Institution Englewood in suburban Denver, Colorado.

How Do You Get on the Ballot to Run for the Presidency as a Candidate of One of the Major Parties?

✳ ✳ ✳

Get Ahold of a Lot of Money

IF YOU ARE NOT wealthy yourself, you need to have a lot of people who are to donate money to your campaign. Running for president is an extraordinarily expensive proposition. And you are running for a long time. So long, in fact, that many candidates run out of money, and then they are out of the race.

As a general rule, many Republicans running for the office obtain financial backing from the business world, including corporations and other interest groups often associated with business and industry.

Democrat hopefuls often receive financial support from unions and labor organizations of many kinds.

The Republican party (also referred to as the Grand Old Party, or GOP) is often considered a probusiness party. The Democratic party is often considered to be proworker (labor).

Both parties receive a great deal of financial support from various celebrities ranging from Oprah (Barrack Obama) to Chuck Norris (Mike Huckabee). Candidates do not invite support from some celebrities (Paris Hilton) that might embarrass their campaign.

It All Begins in Iowa

CANDIDATES FROM THE MAJOR parties (the Republican and Democratic parties) eventually earn the right to become their party's nominee because they have secured the votes of delegates to the convention that is held every four years. These delegates are determined by a state-by-state series of primary elections and caucuses that occur before the convention. In a caucus, people get together and meet and decide which candidate they want to support. The delegates are determined as a result of the votes that occur in these caucuses.

When you vote in a primary election or a caucus, generally, you declare yourself a Republican or Democrat and indicate the person in your party whom you would like to see as your presidential candidate. By indicating the candidate you prefer, you are really electing people who will go to the Republican Convention or Democratic Convention and cast their vote for that candidate. Since these are party affairs, the party rules—not federal rules—are important. People sent to the convention, in some cases, can vote for whomever they want; they may not be bound to vote as the primary election results indicated.

The primary/caucus season begins in the small rural state of Iowa. Iowa is home to about three million people, 91 percent of whom are white—not exactly representative of the US population. As the first state in this primary/caucus selection process, it is of great symbolic importance. Because it is so expensive to campaign in primaries and caucuses, sometimes candidates with a poor showing in Iowa, just the first stop in the selection process, will drop out of the race, usually because their funding (donations) dry up.

The next stop in the selection process is New Hampshire, then South Carolina, followed by Florida and Nevada. Some are caucuses, and some are primary elections. All are for the purpose of electing delegates to either the Republican or Democratic Convention, where the party's nominee is technically selected.

Momentum, a good start, is very important. Sometimes the candidate for the party is pretty much determined by the results of just the first two, three, or four contests.

In effect, then, huge states (such as California) are disenfranchised, because their primary is held quite late in the primary season. This was very surprising to my fellow travelers, who perceived California as being more influential.

Candidates generally require a lot of financial support in the beginning, and a good start. If they have these two things, they can often be successful.

The Hard-Core Party Faithful

THE HARD-CORE PARTY FAITHFUL are generally the ones who vote in these primaries. Often, their views are pretty extreme. The Republicans who participate in voting in these primaries tend to be quite conservative (right wing). The Democrats who vote in these primaries tend to be pretty liberal (left wing). Therefore, it is the extremes in both parties who have a lot of influence in determining who will be the nominee of their party. (In essence, then, extremists often determine a party's nominee, with special weight given to the states that vote early in the primary/caucus process.)

Dirty Tricks

EVEN THOUGH PRIMARIES ARE contested by candidates from the same party, they can be nasty affairs. A candidate's organization will often do "opposition research" on their opponents, bringing any of their personal failings to light and making them public (often by their surrogates so they can deny running a dirty campaign).

Another interesting twist: Let us say that the current president is a Republican, and he is running for reelection for a second four-year term. He will probably not have an opponent in this primary process. This allows Republican voters to declare themselves to be Democrats for this presidential election and support a Democratic candidate they think will be weak in the general election.

The Conventions

THE REPUBLICAN PARTY AND the Democratic party have their conventions. These conventions have different rules, rules that change from convention to convention. It is at these conventions where the delegates actually determine who the party's nominee will be. In recent times, there was no suspense. It was already known who the nominee would be. Also decided at the convention is who the vice presidential candidate will be. Traditionally, the presidential candidate makes this decision at or close to the time of the convention.

The conventions are entertaining. The delegates often wear silly hats; the Republicans wear elephant hats, and the Democrats wear ass hats, as the mascots of the parties are elephants and donkeys (or asses).

This begs the following question: Did the Democrats really think this whole mascot thing through?

At the convention, the parties develop "platforms," their philosophy of what their party should be doing. As a general rule, once a candidate obtains the nomination, he typically ignores this platform (because the platforms are typically the handiwork of the extreme party faithful and tend to be too extreme for the general election, where a lot more people vote). Therefore, in the primaries, candidates try to appeal to the extremes. In the general election, they try to appeal to the middle. The platform is simply a way of rewarding party supporters by recognizing their ideas.

On to the General Election

AFTER THE CONVENTIONS, THE Republican candidate and the Democratic candidate have at it with each other. Things can now really get nasty. Opposition research really kicks in now. If there is something in a candidate's closet, their opponent brings it up continually. If there are no real facts to use against a candidate, their opponent will make negative things up out of whole cloth (e.g., claiming he is really not a US citizen).

Push polls occur just before Election Day. A pollster calls up potential voters, asking realistic questions one would expect an important poll to ask. Then they add a question such as "If the Democratic nominee admitted to having an illegitimate child with a Dominican prostitute, would that change your level of support?" Asking this question sows doubts in the voter's mind. These "polls" tend to occur just before the election, giving the slandered opponent little or no time to respond. Since many voters make up their minds at the last minute, these polls can be devastating to a candidate. These polls are obviously not real but an attempt to impact voter opinion by spreading doubt.

The primary process is easy to defend. I enjoy watching a candidate that is a wealthy urban dweller eating corn dogs at the Iowa State Fair, attempting to court the favor of poor farmers so that they will vote for him in the Iowa caucus. I also enjoy watching convention delegates running around on national television wearing ass hats.

This certainly beats having a king or queen or legislators that wear wigs.

How Do You Get Rid of a President You Do Not Want to Continue in Office?

ANSWER: IMPEACHMENT.

Presidents are elected every four years. In the last 170 years, over one-third of American presidents have become disabled, died in office, or resigned.

Impeachment can lead to a president being kicked out of office. How is this accomplished?

The House of Representatives has a Judiciary Committee that can recommend impeachment.

The committee then studies this recommendation.

If they feel that impeachment is warranted, they send Articles of Impeachment (kind of like an indictment) to the full House of Representatives.

If they send Articles of Impeachment to the House for a vote, the full House of Representatives will write some special rules for taking a vote on the Articles of Impeachment.

The House then votes on the Articles of Impeachment. There may be several of them.

If any one of the Articles of Impeachment is approved by a majority vote of the House of Representatives, the president is then impeached.

This does not mean he is out of office. Not yet.

The president then has a trial, which is held in the Senate. The senators (there are a hundred of them, two from each of the fifty states in the country) are the jury, and the Chief Justice of the Supreme Court acts as the judge. If two thirds of the senators say the president is guilty, out he goes.

Two presidents have been impeached: Andrew Johnson, just after the Civil War, because many senators were not pleased with how he was handling some complicated postwar matters, and Bill Clinton, because he was alleged to have had oral sex with an intern at the White House.

Neither Clinton nor Johnson was ousted from the presidency, because two thirds of the senators did not vote to convict them. Therefore, though both were impeached, neither one was convicted or removed from office, though Clinton was pretty embarrassed (we assume).

There are three interesting things about possible removal from office under these procedures:

1. The process is made possible because it is written into the Constitution. It is one of those "checks and balances" the founders wrote into the Constitution to protect the populace from a corrupt or dangerous person in high office.
2. During the trial in the Senate, the senators who are hearing the case being made must sit silent "under the pain of imprisonment" (if they talk, they could be imprisoned).
3. The Constitution states that a president can be considered for impeachment for treason, bribery, or other high crimes and misdemeanors.

The whole impeachment process compares pretty favorably to coup d'états. One of my fellow train travelers pointed out that former Italian Prime Minister Silvio Berlusconi would certainly have been convicted by the Senate had he been up for an impeachment trial in the United States (out of pure jealousy).

WHO MAKES THE LAWS OF THE COUNTRY?

✳ ✳ ✳

THE CHAMBERS OF THE Congress, the House of Representatives (435 members) and the Senate (100 members), agree as to what the country's laws are. Many members of the House and Senate are trained lawyers, and they write "bills" on an issue; if these bills are passed by both chambers of Congress, they go to the president, who can sign the bill and make it the law of the land. If the president does not sign the bill, that is called a veto and the bill does not become law. The Congress can supersede the president if they pass this bill with a two-thirds majority. Then it is said that Congress "overrode" the veto, and the bill becomes law anyway.

One would think that members of Congress would actually write all the laws, but this is not the case. Very frequently, the actual bills that are introduced to be voted into laws are actually written by the corporations or organizations that are impacted by those laws. They are then given to members of Congress to introduce for a vote.

Members of Congress receive donations from various groups that pass along these proposed bills.

In a famous example, a congressman received many checks from an organization representing the tobacco industry. He passed these campaign donation checks out to representatives on the floor of the

House, prior to a vote on a proposed law that impacted the tobacco industry.

Frequently, when a member of Congress retires, he takes a job with an interest group or industry that he used to regulate when he was in Congress. These organizations hire retired congressmen to try to influence the current members of Congress regarding bills they are considering making into law.

This whole practice is called "lobbying," and the people who do it are called "lobbyists," because in the old days people would hang out in the lobbies of Congress hoping to speak to a congressman on his way to vote on a potential law, in an effort to influence him.

Now they give congressmen checks and do not necessarily hang out in the lobbies.

All this is legal, if not unsavory, and there are some requirements as to how the checks are dispensed: that they are disclosed, and the like.

This practice is easy to defend, because, after all, aren't congressmen entitled to a comfortable retirement too?

Sometimes, the Supreme Court may eventually decide a law, or a part of it, is unconstitutional, thereby negating the action of Congress. This is an example of a "check and balance" the founders wrote into the Constitution, to protect against one branch of government from being too dominant. (There are three branches of government: the executive branch, which includes the president; the judicial branch, which includes the Supreme Court; and the legislative branch, Congress, where the laws are developed.)

WHO TAKES OVER IF SOMETHING HAPPENS TO THE PRESIDENT?

THERE IS AN ORDER of succession that prescribes who comes into power if something terrible happens. The order of succession, and who would take over as president at the time of this writing, are as follows:

#	Office	Current officer
	President of the United States	Barack Obama
1	Vice President of the United States	Joe Biden
2	Speaker of the House	John Boehner
3	President Pro Tempore of the Senate	Daniel Inouye
4	Secretary of State	Hillary Rodham Clinton
5	Secretary of the Treasury	Timothy Geithner
6	Secretary of Defense	Leon Panetta
7	Attorney General	Eric Holder
8	Secretary of the Interior	Ken Salazar
9	Secretary of Agriculture	Tom Vilsack
10	Secretary of Commerce	John Bryson

11	Secretary of Labor	Hilda Solis
12	Secretary of Health and Human Services	Kathleen Sebelius
13	Secretary of Housing and Urban Development	Shaun Donovan
14	Secretary of Transportation	Ray LaHood
15	Secretary of Energy	Steven Chu
16	Secretary of Education	Arne Duncan
17	Secretary of Veterans Affairs	Eric Shinseki
18	Secretary of Homeland Security	Janet Napolitano

The House of Representatives elects the Speaker of the House. He or she is usually, then, a member of the party that is in the majority in that chamber.

The President Pro Tempore of the Senate is the longest serving member of the party that is in the majority in that chamber.

When an event occurs that may involve the attendance of all the people above (such as the president's annual State of the Union address to Congress), one of these people in the line of succession is always sequestered away in a safe, secret, and secure location so that continuity of government is assured if some tragedy befalls those in attendance.

If there is a change of leader, it is handled in accordance with our laws; it is peaceful, noncontroversial, and orderly. Sadly, in many countries, this is not the case. As mean spirited as our politics can be, we do pull together in times of tragedies.

THE IMPORTANCE OF THE SUNDAY MORNING TALK SHOWS IN AMERICAN GOVERNMENT AND POLITICS

✳ ✳ ✳

I WAS ASKED ABOUT the importance of our media.

Every Sunday morning, there are a few high-quality news/talk shows on American television that are extremely important. The quality of the journalism is high. The government does not control these broadcasts in any way.

A couple of examples: *Face the Nation* and *Meet the Press*. These programs have been around longer than most Americans have been alive.

The journalists on these programs are not shills for the government. They really hold the feet of the guests, often American government officials, to the fire, but at the same time, they are respectful. In short, they are old school journalists.

The Sunday morning talk shows have some important functions:

1. The American government communicates to the people through these programs.

A pending crisis in some part of the world may necessitate American involvement. The secretary of state may appear on the program to discuss the situation, answer questions about the crisis, and explain the American government's stance on the issues involved. The program may also be used to "send a message" in an unofficial sense to governments around the world, especially to potential adversaries.

2. Politicians often appear on these programs to explain their ideas on the important issues of the day, apologize or explain past missteps, or float "trial balloons" about a future run for office, policy announcement, and the like. If a guest articulates a policy that receives a critical reception by the press or a bad reaction from the American people, they can revise or totally change their approach.

3. These programs are often used by prominent Americans, often public officials, to reassure the American people, comfort them in times of crisis, or prepare them for some tough going that lies ahead.

4. Often, people may hint at or actually announce that they will be running for office on these programs.

The Sunday morning talk shows are an important, though unofficial, part of the government's dialog with the people. They also allow the American government to make hints to other nations about what lines not to cross, thus averting some misunderstanding or conflict.

Because the journalists involved are willing to take the guests to task, the messages delivered have a unique credibility and carry a great deal of weight.

It is democracy and electronic journalism at its finest.

Many Americans prefer to watch *Seinfeld* reruns, however.

OUR PRESIDENTS ARE
NOT A DULL LOT

✴ ✴ ✴

FOREIGNERS THINK OUR PRESIDENTS are a pretty dull bunch. I disabused them of this notion.

Jimmy Carter claimed that he saw a UFO. Most know he was a peanut farmer. We often forget he also was a nuclear submarine commander.

Calvin Coolidge was commonly known for being a man of few words; what many do not know is that he enjoyed having his head rubbed with petroleum jelly while he ate breakfast in bed.

Gerald Ford was adopted; his name before he was adopted was Leslie Lynch King. He was never elected vice president, he was appointed by Nixon to replace Spiro Agnew (who resigned in disgrace). He was never elected president (he succeeded Nixon, who also resigned in disgrace).

James Garfield could simultaneously write in Latin with one hand while writing in Greek with his other hand. George W. Bush reportedly could write in English with one hand, though some people dispute this.

Warren G. Harding may have been a gambling addict; he lost the White House china in a game of poker.

Andrew Jackson was involved in over a hundred duels. Before being president he was a tailor, and he only wore suits that he had made himself (like Gandhi in some ways, very much not like the Mahatma in others).

In pre-Viagra days, John Tyler had fifteen kids (eight with one wife, seven with another). His last child was born when he was seventy (and we think Bill Clinton was a hound dog).

James Madison never weighed over a hundred pounds, and William Howard Taft was so fat he once became stuck in the White House bathtub.

George Bush, the elder, was responsible for a new word in the Japanese language. The word means to vomit publicly (something Bush famously did once while visiting Japan; he threw up on the Japanese prime minister during a banquet).

John Quincy Adams used to skinny dip in the Potomac River.

Thomas Jefferson had children with his slave, who was a half-sister of his dead wife.

Honest Abe Lincoln was a licensed bartender and was the only US president to own a patent.

Barrack Obama collects *Spiderman* and *Conan the Barbarian* comic books.

MANY NONELECTED PEOPLE HAVE PROFOUNDLY IMPACTED THE UNITED STATES

MY COMPANIONS INQUIRED AS to the influence of people who have not been elected to office.

There are hosts of people who have left their mark on this country; some of them are not household names.

John Hanson was arguably the first president of the United States. He was the president of this newly independent nation under the Articles of Confederation (and yet George Washington's likeness is on the quarter and the dollar bill, and he has the nation's capital and an entire state named after him).

Carrie Nation, a woman in the temperance movement, was very much responsible for the constitutional amendment banning alcohol use in this country. (This amendment was later overturned.)

Ralph Nader, a consumer advocate, saved many lives by pushing for laws that mandated safer cars.

Cesar Chavez, a union advocate for seasonal farm workers, was responsible for many laws that protected these vulnerable people.

Mother Jones worked tirelessly for laws to ensure the safety of mine workers, guard against child labor, protect African American workers' rights, and protect union rights in general.

More Currently

GROVER NORQUIST, A CONSERVATIVE advocate, was able to get many elected Republican officials to take a pledge to not raise taxes for any reason. Those that do not take this public pledge often are not reelected. This pledge hamstrings their ability to be flexible while in office.

Tom Friedman, a *New York Times* columnist, is a frequent guest on the previously discussed influential Sunday morning news programs. His opinions are so respected that he is often deferred to as though he were a head of state.

Fareed Zakaria, a print and electronic journalist, interviews many foreign heads of state that are reluctant to be interviewed on American television. This allows them to express their views to the American public in an informal but effective manner.

Rush Limbaugh, a radio talk show host, is so influential in American conservative circles that high-level elected officials are reluctant to oppose his views and seem to curry his favor. (Currently, his influence seems to be waning, however.)

Ed Schultz, also a radio and television personality, is a strong and influential advocate for "the working man" and "the people that shower after work." He effectively shines a light on any activities that may negatively impact union rights.

And of course, Martin Luther King, Jr. was never a government official, was never elected to office, and had a tremendous positive impact on our nation.

A great thing about America is that you do not have to be in the government, or even extremely wealthy, to have an impact on the nation.

THE UNITED STATES HAS A TWO-PARTY SYSTEM, UNLIKE MANY OTHER COUNTRIES THAT HAVE MULTIPLE PARTIES AND COALITIONS

LIKE OTHER NATIONS, WE have a conservative party (we call them Republicans) and a more liberal or progressive party (the Democrats).

We are similar to other nations in that our liberal party, the Democrats, are considered to be the party of workers and unions, and the conservative party, the Republicans, are considered to be the party of business.

There are some other perceptions that many have of our two parties.

The Republican Party

- considers national defense to be important and believes that we should use the military to influence world events and to support our role as the world's superpower
- advocates for more power for business, less power for unions

- tends to want restrictions on abortion rights
- wants "small government" and lower taxes
- wants to do away with or lessen "entitlements," such as Medicare, Social Security, and unemployment benefits
- believes the "private sector" and "free market" should be virtually unimpeded
- believes, as Ronald Reagan said, "government is the problem, not the solution"
- believes in vouchers, or "school choice"
- is not particularly supportive of gay rights
- believes the private sector is less wasteful than government and can do almost everything better

The Democratic Party

- is viewed as the party of minorities
- supports union rights
- is "pro-choice" on the issue of abortion
- feels that government can play an active role in the economy
- believes that the free market should have restrictions and rules that protect the consumer
- supports public schools
- believes that though national defense is important, we should not be so quick to threaten its use or use it to influence world events, and places emphasis on diplomacy first
- advocates for equal rights for gays
- believes that government can do some things more effectively than the private sector, and that that can be a good thing

What is not readily apparent is this: The Republican party is much better at framing the debate; they coin terms that everyone uses. Since they name the terms, they frame the debate.

The following are terms that Republicans have been successful in getting everyone to use:

Death tax for the estate tax.

Pro-life for abortion restrictions.

Right to work for legislation that restricts workers' rights to organize into unions.

School choice for legislation that allows public money to be spent to send children to private schools if the parents prefer them to public schools. (This underscores Republican support for the private sector over the public sector.)

By coining the terms, the Republicans frame the debate, thus effectively winning many debates before they can even take place.

On the other hand, Democrats can be witty when making a point. For example, a prominent Democratic congressman famously said, "The Republicans support life from conception to birth." (Once you are out of the womb, you are on your own.)

Republicans often seem to be skeptical of science (e.g., they dispute global warming and want creationism taught in schools rather than evolution). Democrats seem more supportive of science.

Both Republicans and Democrats are unsupportive of there being additional political parties. On that, they agree.

All Politics Is Local; Being Elected Has Its Perks

My foreign companions were very impressed with the fact that it is easy to run for office in America. I told them the story of my successful run for a minor elected office.

When I was quite young, I was approached by a number of teachers from my children's school to run for the local school board. I was viewed (and rightfully so) as being "proteacher" because I have a great deal of respect for educators and a lot of appreciation for what they were doing for my children. So I ran for office.

I was elected and served two terms. I was amazed at the respect elected officials have in our country, and the vast majority of them are public servants for the right reasons: to make the country a better place.

Americans trust the election process, and those that run are generally respected and appreciated for their efforts (especially when they serve in a nonpaying position, as I did).

One of the perks of my election: my children tended to be assigned to the best teachers. A coincidence?

I am grateful to live in a country where people could feel comfortable in approaching me to run, and that the whole election process was transparent and, in a sense, sacred, something that people took very seriously.

And it was sure a nice thing that my kids had great teachers for eight years.

Such opportunities to serve are not so readily available in other countries, I learned. My traveling companions expressed a hope that such opportunities would become more readily available in their countries. They viewed this as a very positive thing.

WHAT IS POSSE COMITATUS
(AND WHY IS IT IMPORTANT)?
✳ ✳ ✳

MY TRAVELING COMPANIONS HAD a number of questions about the place of the military in American government and politics. This prompted a discussion of *posse comitatus*.

This law and concept was a surprise to my European friends and may be news to many Americans. It is something that makes our country fundamentally different from many others.

In 1878, Congress passed a law that essentially prohibited the US Army from engaging in local law enforcement activities unless those activities were authorized by Congress or the Constitution. Later, the navy and air force were also prohibited from such activities. (Though technically one of our armed forces, the coast guard has no such prohibition.)

In many nations, even Western-style democracies, no such prohibition exists. This is an important safeguard for a free people and a long-standing tradition in our country.

In many nations, there is always a lingering, albeit mild, fear that the military may take some action to influence the political events of the country. This is not a concern in the United States.

Additionally, our nation has a time-honored tradition that the military is under civilian control. The Constitution mandates this civilian control. This is a characteristic of our country that should never be taken for granted.

Soldiers based at our domestic military bases do not carry weapons unless they are actually training. Security at these bases is actually handled by a police force. This underscores that our military is in place to protect the nation from foreign adversaries, not to control it or have any influence on the civilian government or the populace.

In few countries around the world would a head of state feel comfortable enough to warn its people to be wary of the influence of the military-industrial complex, as President Dwight D. Eisenhower famously did.

Civilian control of the military is a distinction that differentiates our nation from others and is as impressive as it is important.

Those in our armed forces do not swear allegiance to a king, queen, or president. They swear to protect the Constitution. They also commit to follow all *lawful* orders.

THE FIRST LADY AND HER CAUSE

★ ★ ★

A NUMBER OF QUESTIONS were asked about the role of the president's spouse.

The president's wife (we have yet to have a president's husband) is referred to as "the First Lady." The First Lady is not an official position and has no salary, though she does have an office in the White House and a staff. She has no official duties or powers (except privately over the president, but that is another story).

Though a First Lady has no official powers or duties, she does have considerable influence on a variety of issues, primarily due to whatever cause she adopts as her area of interest and concern.

In recent times, First Ladies have embraced causes that are as uncontroversial as possible, and are near and dear to their hearts. Often, their advocacy can lead to attention that may prompt positive changes. This tradition is generally viewed as positive.

Lyndon Johnson's wife, Lady Bird, promoted environmental protection and beautification. Pat Nixon advocated for volunteerism. Rosalyn Carter put a spotlight on the needs of the mentally disabled. Betty Ford was a strong advocate for women's rights, and her courage displayed in her battle with alcoholism helped remove the stigma associated with the disease and encouraged many to seek help. Laura Bush supported literacy (some cynically suggested this was because her husband could not read). The current First Lady, Michelle Obama, has brought attention to the epidemic of childhood obesity.

Todd Palin, the husband of former Alaska Governor Sarah Palin (who was John McCain's vice presidential running mate in 2008) referred to himself as "the First Dude" when his wife served as governor.

When we finally have a female president, I hope her husband does not take Todd Palin's lead.

Though we have never had a female president, some historians may argue this point. Woodrow Wilson suffered a stroke while president. While recovering, his wife would emerge from his bedroom to proclaim her husband's orders, pronouncements, and opinions. No one was ever sure if these decisions were his or hers.

The First Ladies' causes reflect well on the country and are a uniquely American tradition well respected overseas. Domestically, they help a lot of people.

SEPARATION OF CHURCH
AND STATE: NOT SO MUCH
✳ ✳ ✳

I WAS ASKED ABOUT the role of the church in American politics and government.

Much is made over the separation of church and state in the United States. Indeed, the First Amendment to the Constitution is this: "Congress shall make no law respecting an establishment of religion, or prohibiting the free exercise thereof; or abridging the freedom of speech, or of the press; or the right of the people peaceably to assemble, and to petition the Government for a redress of grievances."

This separation of church and state is not so prevalent in other democracies. Many modern democracies have a state religion; in some democratic countries, the head of state is considered to be the head of the church. In Denmark, the government collects taxes and directs them to the state church.

The United States seems to have a firewall between church and state, that is one characteristic of our country foreigners often point out and ask about. But is that accurate?

John Witherspoon, a clergyman, was one of the signers of the Declaration of Independence.

Our national motto (since 1956) is "In God We Trust."

Every session of the Supreme Court is opened by a crier saying, "God save the United States and this honorable Court" (ironically, the Supreme Court has ruled against prayer in school).

Father Patrick Conroy, a priest, is the sixtieth chaplain of the House of Representatives.

Mike Huckabee, a former governor of Arkansas and a Baptist preacher, made a serious run for the Republican nomination for the presidency.

John Anderson, a twenty-year member of the House of Representatives, and an Independent candidate for the presidency in 1980, introduced legislation for a constitutional amendment to "Recognize the authority of Jesus Christ over the United States." (Anderson, before becoming a congressman, was a lawyer. Presumably, he studied the First Amendment while working towards his JD, yet he proposed a JC amendment).

Any US president that did not end an address to the nation with "May God bless you, and may God bless the United States of America" would have a political shelf life about as long as a US president that did not utter "so help me God" after taking the oath of office for the presidency (not so long).

Billy Graham, a prominent pastor, served as confidant and adviser to many presidents.

Congress itself is responsible for many people praying. But that is another story.

The Importance of the Press; The Importance of "-Gates"

My seatmates were very interested in American political scandals and why we always refer to them with a "-gate" suffix.

The First Amendment to the Constitution guarantees freedom of the press, something people around the world admire and certainly seek to establish if their country does not have it.

A free press is important not just because a democracy is not really vibrant or feasible without it, but because it serves as a check against government wrongdoing and abuse of power; in essence, it protects the people from an overreaching government.

The "watchdog" function of a free press has highlighted and curbed government wrongdoing at both the local and national level. Coming from Chicago, I can appreciate this. A free press, in essence, keeps a government honest. This function is so vital that some refer to the press as the "fourth branch" of our democracy.

A good press drives home the point that those in power, while they may be entitled to their own opinions, are not entitled to their own facts.

A free, investigative press deters improper governmental behavior and wrongdoing.

At the national level, the most prominent example is the Watergate scandal, which brought to light some serious governmental wrongdoing that eventually led to President Nixon's resignation (the Watergate Hotel complex was where the Democratic National Committee's offices were located).

Ever since the Watergate episode in American history, major political scandals uncovered by journalists have often had the suffix "-gate" attached to them. For example:

Irangate (also referred to as "Contragate")—The Reagan administration illegally sold weapons to Iran to raise revenue to purchase weapons that were then illegally sold to rebels in Nicaragua.

Monicagate (a.k.a. Zippergate)—President Clinton's "improper" relationship with Monica Lewinsky.

Filegate—The illegal possession of hundreds of FBI files by the Clinton White House.

Government officials want a "-gate" suffix attached to one of their actions about as much as they want to see a *60 Minutes* crew in their waiting room.

In our country, investigative journalists win prizes and become heroes. In much of the rest of the world, they are executed.

You have to love this freedom of the press thing.

He Whose Name Must Not Be Spoken: We Have No Voldemorts

When traveling in Germany, I learned that in some countries there are some people's names that literally must not be spoken. Seriously, you do not say the "H-word" in Germany. You can actually go to jail if you say, "Heil H*****." (Unless you are a foreigner. A German citizen will go to jail. You will not.)

I realize we have had some bad actors, or "evil doers" as Dubya would say, but none so bad that his name cannot be spoken. Sure, Benedict Arnold was not one of our most beloved historical figures, but we can say his name. Senator Joe McCarthy was so bad that his name spawned a term, "McCarthyism," which basically means the destruction of someone's life by making false accusations, as McCarthy did when he accused so many people of being Communists during the "Red scare" years—knowing full well they were not really Communists, and ruining their lives, even driving some to suicide.

Heck, in Chicago, we will even say aloud the name of the current manager of the Chicago Cubs.

We are truly lucky that we have no Voldemorts. And people in other countries are jealous.

The American Dream

The most interesting thing I was asked to do was to define "the American Dream."

There is some argument as to what constitutes the American Dream. Some feel it is owning your own home, having two cars, and being able to take a vacation every year. Others feel it is providing your children with a better life than you had.

I learned that the American Dream to those that live abroad is immigrating to America and becoming a US citizen. That dream is as prevalent today as it was two hundred years ago.

AMERICAN EXCEPTIONALISM

AMERICAN POLITICIANS, ESPECIALLY THOSE running for president, like to sound off about American Exceptionalism. To some, it means that America is to be judged by a different standard, that it does no wrong. That it is the world's most formidable military power and has the right to do whatever it pleases because it is morally superior. Speaking about American Exceptionalism seems to be a prerequisite for running for the highest office in our country. Those that speak about it seem to believe that they can will it into existence if they shout about it loud enough.

Our current president has stated that he believes in American Exceptionalism, much as a French leader believes in French Exceptionalism, or a Swedish prime minister believes in Swedish Exceptionalism. Some think that his saying that is a bad thing.

I believe this:

That a country where an African American man from humble beginnings, from a single-parent home, whose absentee father came from Africa, who was basically raised by his grandparents who were not wealthy, could be elected president is exceptional.

This president now lives in the White House, a structure that was originally built with slave labor.

That is American Exceptionalism.

Name me another country where that could happen.

Our Constitution Specifically Tells Us What to Do about Pirates. Who Says It Is Outdated?

Our conversation briefly left American government and politics and drifted to a conversation of pirates, a subject very important to Europeans. I was able to share with them that our Constitution actually addresses the problem of piracy.

Article 1, Section 8, of the Constitution specifically addresses the problem of pirates. Talk about a document that stands the test of time! This particular section of the Constitution talks about the powers of the Congress, one of which is that they can issue letters of marque and reprisal.

A letter of marque can be issued by a nation to a privateer or mercenary to act on behalf of that nation for the purpose of retaliating against another nation for some wrong, such as a border incursion or seizure.

Reprisal is an act taken by a nation, short of war, to gain redress for an action taken against that nation. For example, seizing a ship in retaliation for a seized ship.

Congress, then, not only has the power to declare war, it can go after pirates in a limited way, without even utilizing US forces in the process. The added bonus is it is constitutional.

Not good for some Somalis, Jack Sparrow, or a certain guy with a black beard.

THE CLOWN CIRCUS

DEFENDING THE FIELD OF potential GOP candidates for president was no small task. Foreigners have a surprising amount of knowledge about the people who may be running, whereas I cannot even name the president of Ubeki-beki-beki-beki-stan-stan.

Here is a list of potential candidates we discussed, some interesting things about them, and my defense of them (I did point out that the only requirements to be president are that you are thirty-five years old and that you were born in the United States):

1. Donald Trump (a.k.a. "The Donald")
- He is the son of a real-estate investor and is a real-estate investor himself.
- He's very wealthy.
- He has a unique head of hair.
- He has participated in many World Wrestling Entertainment events.
- He's the owner of casinos.
- Some of his properties had difficulty with bankruptcy.
- He's the star of the television show *The Apprentice* and is known for his catch phrase "You're fired."
- He claims he sent investigators to Hawaii to look into President Obama's birth certificate.

- He owns the Miss America pageant and other beauty pageants.
- He had a feud with Rosie O'Donnell.

My defense: his detractors are jealous of his hair, money, and access to good-looking women.

2. Herman Cain
- He's a former CEO of a Mafia-themed pizza chain.

My defense: What's not to like?

3. Newt Gingrich
- He's a former Speaker of the House of Representatives.
- He was fined a substantial amount of money for ethics violations while serving in Congress as Speaker.
- He's happily married.
- He's married to the woman he was having an affair with when married to his previous wife.
- His first wife was his high school teacher who saw his potential.
- He led the charge for President Clinton's impeachment because President Clinton was putting his tallywhacker where it did not belong.
- While leading the impeachment effort against Clinton, he was having an affair and presumably had his tallywhacker in places it should not have been.

My defense: This man lived every high school student's dream. Leave him alone (this added a lot of levity to our discussion).

4. Mitt Romney
- He's rumored to wear "magic underwear." (Prominent Mormons are believed to be given special undergarments that protect them from evil, and he is a prominent Mormon. Not that there is anything wrong with that.)

- His father was born in Mexico, where his grandfather fled due to "religious persecution." (His grandfather had a few wives, simultaneously.)

My defense: It is about time we had a Hispanic president. Having a president named Mitt would show how far we have come as a country. Mitt is so darned good looking.

5. Rick Santorum
- He had a child who, sadly, died at the hospital. He and his wife decided to bring the dead baby home to meet the siblings.

My defense: I could not defend or condemn this act, but I did say that Santorum by far was the best candidate in either party to Google. (I then explained Santorum's "Google problem.")

6. Michelle Bachman
Here is a hit parade of famous Michelle Bachman quotes:

1. "I don't know how much God has to do to get the attention of the politicians. We've had an earthquake; we've had a hurricane. He said, 'Are you going to start listening to me here?' Listen to the American people because the American people are roaring right now. They know government is on a morbid obesity diet and we've got to rein in the spending."
2. "Well, what I want them to know is just like John Wayne was from Waterloo, Iowa. That's the kind of spirit that I have, too." (Bachman thought she was talking about the beloved American actor, John Wayne. But it was John Wayne Gacy, a notorious serial killer, who was born in Waterloo, Iowa.)
3. "I will tell you that I had a mother last night come up to me here in Tampa, Florida, after the debate. She told me that her little daughter took that vaccine, that injection,

and she suffered from mental retardation thereafter." (Bachman was talking about the HPV vaccine. No evidence supports this claim, and no one could locate the woman who supposedly said this.)

4. "Why should I go and do something like that? But the Lord says, 'Be submissive wives; you are to be submissive to your husbands.'" (She said this when explaining why she went into tax law as a profession. Her husband told her to, and she thought God was speaking through her husband.)

5. "I wish the American media would take a great look at the views of the people in Congress and find out: Are they pro-America or anti-America?" (Where have you gone, Joe McCarthy, our nation turns its lonely eyes to you, woo woo woo.)

6. "I find it interesting that it was back in the 1970s that the swine flu broke out then under another Democrat president, Jimmy Carter. And I'm not blaming this on President Obama, I just think it's an interesting coincidence." (On the 1976 swine flu outbreak that actually happened when Gerald Ford, a Republican, was president.)

7. "Carbon dioxide is portrayed as harmful. But there isn't even one study that can be produced that shows that carbon dioxide is a harmful gas." Okay …

8. "Before we get started, let's all say 'Happy Birthday' to Elvis Presley today." She said this while campaigning on the anniversary of Elvis's death.

My defense: Actually, I cannot defend her. Anyone who mocks Elvis's death cannot be trusted. He or she should not have his or her finger on the nuclear trigger.

9. At a campaign stop in New Hampshire, Bachman mentioned that the famous battles of the Revolutionary War at Lexington and Concord were fought in that

state. (Even the Europeans in my train car knew that they were fought in Massachusetts, because they learned that in history classes that they took in high school.)

My defense: A lot of people do not know where those two battles were fought.

Michelle, why did you decide not to run in 2012? We miss your grasp of the facts.

THE SOUTHERN STRATEGY

I WAS ASKED IF there were any concepts that were important in American politics that foreigners may not be aware of. This gave me an opportunity to discuss "the Southern Strategy."

For years, the southern states reliably voted Democratic, so much so that Democrats referred to it as "the solid South."

The Democratic party worked very hard to pass civil rights laws, culminating in a Voting Rights Act that protected the voting rights of minorities.

The Republican party, seeking to capitalize on and exploit white fears, played on these fears to appeal to southern white voters. This strategy was credited to two Republican presidential candidates, Barry Goldwater and Richard Nixon.

Since the advent of this strategy, the solid South remains solid, but now for Republicans, not Democrats.

This huge change in American politics has serious ramifications in national elections even today.

Those traveling with me were not aware of this, and I am glad they were not.

We Have a Lot of Political Scandals, and They Usually Do Not Involve Sex

My fellow professors could not get enough of American scandals. They asked for a little historical perspective on our major scandals and were surprised that many of them were not related to sex.

The Teapot Dome Scandal (1922–1924)

This is the first scandal American schoolkids read about in their history books. Usually they do not understand it.

President Taft reserved an oil field in Wyoming for the US Navy to tap in times of emergency. Taft's secretary of the interior, Albert Fall, was involved in the leasing of these oil fields under questionable circumstances. Fall received substantial gifts connected to these leases. The *Wall Street Journal* broke the story, and the Congress investigated it.

Watergate (1972–1974, but with permanent impact)

This is the granddaddy of all American scandals and always will be. Ever since Watergate, any big scandal has the suffix "-gate" attached to it by the American press.

The Watergate scandal basically involved some Nixon supporters engaging in illegal acts in an attempt to help his reelection campaign.

A group of Nixon supporters broke into the offices of the Democratic National Committee (which was located in the Watergate Hotel complex in Washington, DC) to obtain information that might assist the Nixon campaign in the upcoming presidential election. Some of the burglars were ex-CIA agents; one was a former district attorney. A security guard noticed their second break-in at this facility and called the police. The arrest of these burglars led to an investigation that eventually caused President Nixon to resign, the first president in American history to do so.

The president was implicated in this scandal by tapes that were recorded at the White House. A secret source called "Deep Throat" fed information to a couple of newspaper reporters that kept the story alive, prompted impeachment hearings by the Congress, and eventually resulted in Nixon's resigning in disgrace (before he could be impeached).

This scandal demonstrated two remarkable things:

1. It demonstrated the importance of a free press in keeping government honest.
2. It showed that no man is above the law in our country, not even the president.

(It should be noted that prior to the Watergate scandal, Nixon's vice president, Spiro Agnew, had resigned in disgrace due to a bribery scandal that had its beginnings when Agnew was the governor of Maryland, prior to becoming Nixon's vice president.)

Nixon and Agnew may have been the original "dynamic duo."

The Keating Five (1989)

THE COLLAPSE OF A large savings and loan outfit, called the Lincoln Savings and Loan Association, ended up costing the government billions of dollars.

Five senators were accused of asking a government investigator that was looking into the collapse of Lincoln Savings and Loan to "back off." The five accused senators had received substantial campaign contributions from the president of this savings and loan, Mr. Charles Keating.

Downing Street Memo

THIS SCANDAL SPANNED TWO continents and the Atlantic Ocean.

The *London Times* discovered a memo that indicated George W. Bush was going to put out false information about Saddam Hussein's weapons of mass destruction. This was going to be done to make a case for war against Iran.

This story received a lot of play in the press in the UK, but not so much in the United States.

We ended up going to war with Iran.

The Pentagon Papers

DANIEL ELLSBERG, A MILITARY analyst and former Pentagon consultant, leaked a number of classified papers to the *New York Times*, documents that strongly indicated that the Vietnam War was unwinnable. These papers also demonstrated that the American public was being deceived about the war.

These leaks contributed a great deal to the ending of the war and the American public's dissatisfaction with it.

The government went to the Supreme Court in an attempt to restrain the *New York Times* from printing these leaked documents.

The Supreme Court ruled that the *New York Times* could go ahead and publish the papers.

Like the Watergate scandal, the Pentagon Papers scandal highlighted the importance of a free and independent press in keeping the government honest and in informing the public.

Monicagate

YES, LIKE EUROPE, WE have our sex scandals.

When another matter was being investigated, it was discovered that President Clinton had an inappropriate relationship with a female intern, Monica Lewinsky. While under oath, Clinton did not tell the truth about this relationship. This resulted in his impeachment, something that my European friends could not understand.

Clinton was very popular abroad and pretty popular at home as well. The actions of Congress were bewildering to many people.

Wikileaks (Ongoing)

HOW COULD A LOWLY soldier allegedly obtain extremely sensitive US government secrets and leak them, doing untold damage to US relations with many countries, and actually putting many lives at risk?

This scandal, and its implications, has yet to play out.

Take-Away from These Scandals

PEOPLE ARE GENERALLY HELD accountable, even if they are in the government. Our free press is essential in getting out the truth.

The world, for the most part, sees our "airing of the dirty laundry" to be a sign of strength and national character. Our transparent nature, and our free press, is much admired by the world.

THE GI BILL

* * *

I WAS ASKED IF we had put in place some good, transformational laws. This prompted a discussion of the GI bill.

When our troops returned from World War II, the nation looked for a small way to partially compensate them for the great sacrifices they had made on our behalf, a way to say thanks and a mechanism to ease their reintegration into American life.

Congress passed the GI bill to do this. What is lost in history is that the GI bill benefited the country as a whole, more than just the veterans it was meant to thank.

The GI bill provided education benefits that allowed many World War II veterans to earn college degrees. The result: we became the most educated people the world has ever seen. These educated veterans, as a result of this training, were able to make great contributions to art, science, and industry.

These contributions, which would not have occurred without these trained and educated veterans, changed our country and changed the world.

The United States became the world leader in many fields because of the talents and training of those helped by the GI bill.

In essence, the veterans served us capably twice.

My fellow travelers were perplexed as to why we were not still doing this. So am I.

THE MEN WHO WOULD BE KING (BUT NEVER RAN)

✳ ✳ ✳

I WAS ASKED IF there were some people who could have "ascended to the throne" but chose not to.

We have had some politicians in our history who never ran for the highest office but were thought to be "shoo-ins" if they did.

Colin Powell, military hero, secretary of state from 2001 to 2005, chairman of the Joint Chiefs of Staff (the nation's top military officer) from 1989 to 1993, and national security adviser from 1987 to 1989, was widely admired; he was seen as apolitical by many (a plus) and a genuine hero. Polls suggested he could have obtained either party's nomination. He never ran.

Mario Cuomo, governor of New York from 1983 to 1994, seen by people from all sides of the political spectrum as being exceptionally competent, also never ran.

Generally, in our nation, it is fairly easy to catch "Potomac Fever." But a few have not succumbed.

THE BABY BOOMERS
✳ ✳ ✳

THE BABY BOOM GENERATION (people born to American families after World War II, between 1946 and 1964) was the biggest demographic blip in our nation's history. As they progressed through their life span, what was important to them became important to the nation. Due to their numbers, their influence has always been felt. Elementary education, college, health care, and now retirement have all become serious issues as the boomers have progressed.

The generation preceding them, the "Greatest Generation," was credited for winning World War II and making the world safe and free. Their offspring, the boomers, can rightfully take pride in working for progress in the areas of civil rights as well as gender, racial, and religious equality.

Not too shabby.

GAYS, GUNS, AND GOD
✵ ✵ ✵

IN AMERICAN POLITICS, ONE way to rally the troops, increase incoming campaign donations, and possibly distract from issues you may not want to address is to discuss gays, guns, and God. Using these "wedge issues" has become an art form with some Republican candidates. In general, their feelings tend to be as follows:

God: For. Big time.

Gays: Against. They seem to be the cause of so many problems.

Guns: Everybody should have one, and they should not be restricted in any way.

The Road to the White House Runs through David Letterman's Studio

✳ ✳ ✳

OUR DISCUSSION OF THE American media and its importance continued. Many of our TV programs are televised in Europe.

David Letterman once suggested that no one could be elected to the nation's highest office unless they first appeared on his program. This may be true. American politicians need to show that they are one of us. They do this by wearing jeans when they campaign and by appearing on popular television shows. Nixon famously appeared on *Laugh-In*, stuck his head out a window in the opening segment, and said, "Sock it to me" (he probably never watched *Laugh-In*). Clinton played the saxophone on *The Tonight Show* with Jay Leno, and Letterman shamed John McCain into making up for a canceled appearance on his show. Why? Because the road to the White House runs through David Letterman's Ed Sullivan Theatre.

SILLY SEASON

THERE ARE SOME GREAT traditions at the highest level of our government. The president usually greets professional and college championship teams at the White House. He will also attend the annual Gridiron Dinner and the White House Correspondents' Dinner, where all the powerful are roasted, including the president. The president always gets an opportunity to give as well as he takes. It is all in good fun and uniquely American. Such comedy in other countries directed toward the commander-in-chief might lead to a beheading or two. Here is my favorite tradition: every year on Thanksgiving, the president commutes a turkey's sentence and frees it to live out its life on a nearby farm instead of becoming someone's dinner.

As the great American Yakov Smirnoff would say: "Only in America. What a country."

I agree.

AFTERWORD

OFTEN, IT IS DIFFICULT, if not misleading, to attempt to explain a complex subject in very simple terms. When we try to boil something down, we often end up boiling it away.

One can explain American government and politics in simple terms and do so accurately. This simplification is accurate, is not taught in schools, and is not much talked about.

The simple explanation of American politics and government is this:

The most important number in American government and politics is five.

IT TAKES FIVE VOTES on the Supreme Court to determine if a law stands, if it is, indeed, the law of the land. Whether it is an issue of free speech, abortion, who can own guns, who can be incarcerated without benefit of a trial, or when recounts end when we are attempting to decide who the next president of the United States should be, it all comes down to five.

Five people in robes. We can only hope that they get it right.